T. LAM

# The Etsy Seller's Secret Weapon

*Crack The Etsy Algorithm and Boost Your Sales for Less Than a Cup of Coffee*

Copyright © 2024 by T. Lam

All rights reserved. No part of this publication may be reproduced, stored or transmitted in any form or by any means, electronic, mechanical, photocopying, recording, scanning, or otherwise without written permission from the publisher. It is illegal to copy this book, post it to a website, or distribute it by any other means without permission.

T. Lam asserts the moral right to be identified as the author of this work.

T. Lam has no responsibility for the persistence or accuracy of URLs for external or third-party Internet Websites referred to in this publication and does not guarantee that any content on such Websites is, or will remain, accurate or appropriate.

Designations used by companies to distinguish their products are often claimed as trademarks. All brand names and product names used in this book and on its cover are trade names, service marks, trademarks and registered trademarks of their respective owners. The publishers and the book are not associated with any product or vendor mentioned in this book. None of the companies referenced within the book have endorsed the book.

First edition

This book was professionally typeset on Reedsy.
Find out more at reedsy.com

# Contents

| | |
|---|---|
| Introduction | 1 |
| Chapter 1: Your Etsy Listings - From Invisible to... | 3 |
| Chapter 2: Important Key Etsy Stats | 7 |
| Chapter 3: The Etsy Brain - Decoding Etsy's Search Algorithm | 13 |
| Chapter 4: Relevance | 16 |
| Chapter 5: Quality and Customer & Market Experience Score | 20 |
| Chapter 6: Recency of Listings and Listing Age | 24 |
| Chapter 7: Shipping Price | 28 |
| Chapter 8: Conversion Rate | 30 |
| Chapter 9: The Secret Weapon | 35 |
| Conclusion: The Journey Continues | 42 |
| Resources | 45 |

# Introduction

Welcome to The Etsy Seller's Secret Weapon book, your step-by-step guide to transforming your Etsy shop into a successful and thriving business. This book is not for you if you are trying to figure out how to open your first Etsy shop. You can find plenty of helpful info online for that. This book is for Etsy shop sellers who already have a few active Etsy listings but are struggling to get any traction or looking to scale up. I've walked the same path, faced the same frustrations, and I'm here to share with you what I've discovered—secrets that have helped me and others take our shops from invisible to profitable, in a matter of weeks, not months, not years.

Etsy can feel like a crowded marketplace where only a few listings seem to shine. You might find yourself asking: *Why aren't my products being found? What am I doing wrong?* If you're reading this, you've probably already tried several strategies with limited success. I was once in your shoes—running a shop that barely made sales, trying to figure out why others were succeeding while I was struggling to get noticed.

The truth is, simply listing a great product on Etsy isn't enough. It's not just about having a creative product line; it's about mastering the science behind Etsy's search algorithm, optimizing your shop, and learning how to drive traffic. That's where The Etsy Seller's Secret Weapon comes into play. This strategy helped me boost my shop from average sales to explosive growth. I didn't have a huge marketing budget or fancy degrees in business. What I did have was the determination to figure out what really works on Etsy, and I'm here to share those insights with you.

**What to Expect**

This isn't just another book full of generic advice. Every chapter is packed with specific, actionable steps that you can take immediately to start seeing real results in your shop. We'll cover everything from optimizing your product listings to leveraging Etsy's search algorithm, and I'll walk you through each step of the Secret Weapon strategy. By the end of this book, you'll have a complete roadmap for growing your Etsy shop, boosting your visibility, and turning your listings into consistent revenue generators.

You don't need a big budget or advanced marketing skills to succeed on Etsy. What you do need is the right strategy, the willingness to take action, and the patience to see it through. If you're ready to finally break through and take your Etsy shop to new heights, let's get started.

Your journey to Etsy success starts here.

# Chapter 1: Your Etsy Listings - From Invisible to Irresistible

Before we dive into the heart of the Etsy algorithm, take note of the insights you'll find in the brackets [ ]. These side notes, sprinkled throughout the book, come from my personal experiences and the hard-earned lessons I've gathered from my Etsy journey. Through trial, error, and a bit of unconventional testing, you'll see how I went from barely making a few dollars a month to eventually leaving my full-time job to run my Etsy shop full-time. While Etsy's algorithm and shopping trends may change over time, the strategies I'm about to share have consistently proven effective throughout my 10 years of selling on the platform. This book also contains simple, **actionable steps** that will not only help your shop succeed but also ensure long-term success.

**Great Products Won't Sell Themselves**

Imagine you're crafting a beautiful product, pouring hours of creativity and effort into it, but when you put it up for sale, it doesn't attract the attention you expected. This can be disheartening, but often, the issue isn't the product itself—it's that the right people aren't seeing it. Opening your store and marketing an online shop without optimizing it is like casting a wide net into the ocean, hoping to catch the right fish. It's inefficient and can lead to wasted time and resources.

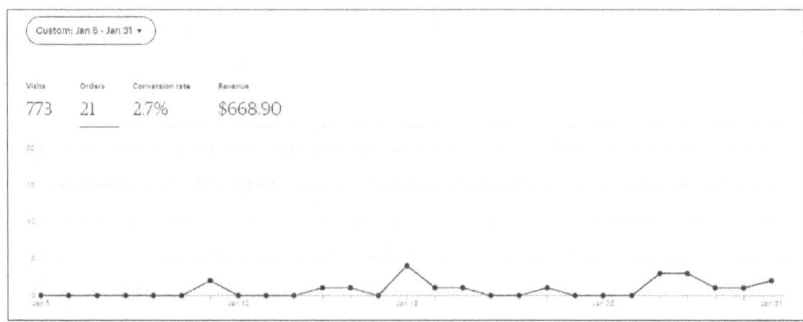

*Figure 1*

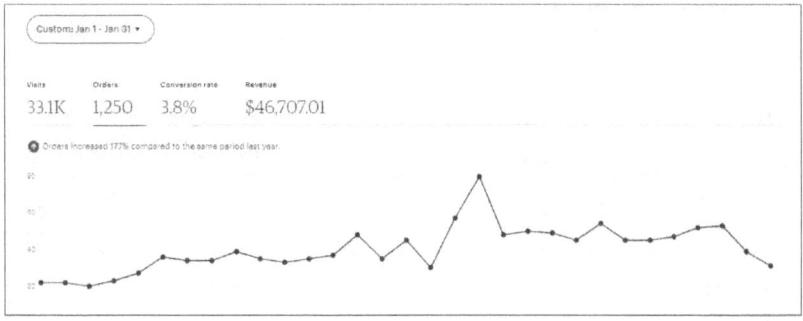

*Figure 2*

Take a look at these two Etsy graphs comparing a shop's stats between year 1 (Figure 1) and year 2 (Figure 2). Figure 1 demonstrates a shop's dismal performance before any optimization or marketing. In contrast, Figure 2 highlights the shop's rapid growth after applying the strategy you're about to learn in this book. This shop went from virtually invisible to irresistible in no time.

CHAPTER 1: YOUR ETSY LISTINGS - FROM INVISIBLE TO...

*[ "The right people aren't seeing it" was the slogan for my Etsy shop. I quickly realized, after I had opened my first Etsy store, that I had no idea what I was doing. I rushed to list my products, thinking they would naturally attract buyers. My mindset was, 'If I build it, they will come.' But that couldn't have been further from the truth. My titles weren't optimized, and I didn't use consistent tags—basic things I didn't even think about. It didn't take long to realize that while there was a huge audience on Etsy who would love my products, they didn't know I existed. I began to understand that just like I discovered things I didn't know I needed as a buyer, my potential customers couldn't find me because my shop wasn't optimized for traffic. ]*

## Here are 10 essential Etsy Tips to optimize your Etsy shop's listings for better visibility:

- **Use Relevant Keywords in Titles and Tags:** Ensure your product titles and tags include popular, relevant search terms to match buyer queries.

*[ Relevant keywords in titles and tags are absolutely essential before any marketing strategy is undertaken. I accidentally discovered generic keyword phrases that generated a lot more traffic to my shop. I explain this further in Chapter 4. ]*

- **Maximize Title Characters:** Use the full 140-character limit for your titles to include multiple relevant keywords.
- **Optimize Product Descriptions:** Write clear, detailed descriptions that include key phrases customers might search for.
- **Select Accurate Categories and Attributes:** Choose the most appropriate categories and product attributes to help Etsy correctly match your items in search results.
- **Upload High-Quality Photos:** Use multiple, high-resolution

images that show your product from different angles and in different contexts.
- **Use Etsy's Search Suggestions:** Leverage Etsy's autocomplete tool to discover popular search phrases and incorporate them into your listings.
- **Offer Free Shipping:** Listings with free shipping tend to rank higher in Etsy search results, as Etsy prioritizes them.
- **Renew Listings Regularly:** Refresh your listings by renewing them or making updates to maintain their relevance.
- **Encourage Customer Reviews:** Positive reviews contribute to your shop's reputation and can boost listing visibility.
- **Analyze Competitors' Listings:** Study successful competitors to identify keyword strategies and trends that may work for your shop.

Implementing these optimization techniques will improve your chances of ranking higher in Etsy's search results and attracting more potential buyers. In the following chapters we will laser-focus our attention on a few of these essential tips.

# Chapter 2: Important Key Etsy Stats

Understanding key Etsy statistics is crucial for making smart decisions and setting realistic goals. For example, knowing that 74% of Etsy businesses eventually fail puts into perspective just how competitive and tough the market is. However, with the right strategy, you can defy the odds. I was once part of that 74%, but my story didn't end there. These stats emphasize the importance of having a solid approach to be seen in such a competitive marketplace. In this chapter, we'll explore important data—from user demographics to conversion rates—to help you gain a better understanding of the landscape.

- Number of sellers: Etsy had over 9 million sellers in 2023, a 21% increase from 2022.
- Number of buyers: Etsy had 96.48 million active buyers in 2023, a 1.5% increase from 2022.
- Revenue: Etsy generated $2.74 billion in revenue in 2023, a 7% increase from 2022.

[ *A lot of people worry about selling online because they think, 'The market is too crowded,' or 'Everyone's already selling this.' My response is simple: even if you're the only one selling a product, it won't matter if people can't find you* or don't know your shop exists. The same goes for sellers offering something popular, like personalized tumblers. If they don't know how to show up on the first few pages of Etsy search results, it doesn't matter how many others are selling it. This book is here to help you get your listings onto those first pages, no matter how much competition is out there. ]

**What is a good Etsy conversion rate:**

- 1-2%: If your shop is new or you're selling in a highly competitive category, a 1-2% conversion rate might be what you initially see.
- 3-5%: This is considered a strong conversion rate and indicates that your shop is performing well.
- Above 5%: Signifies exceptional effectiveness in attracting the right visitors to your Etsy shop and converting those visits into purchases.

[ It's not just about having a good conversion rate. Even if your conversion rate is above average, like 3% or higher, you won't make much money without enough traffic. My sister's shop early on had a solid 4% conversion rate but only had 1.8K monthly views. After I stepped in and applied a few key optimization strategies, including The Etsy Seller's Secret Weapon, her conversion rate only went up by 1%, from 4% to 5%. However, her traffic surged to 8.8K views per month. That 5% conversion on 8.8K visits resulted in a significant boost in her revenue. Her sales skyrocketed by 617%. The takeaway? It's crucial to optimize your listings to drive more clicks and traffic—sales will follow. ]

- 74% of all Etsy businesses eventually fail.
- The average Etsy seller earns between $43,000 and $46,000 annually.
- Average Etsy seller makes $2,900 per year, top earners $65,000 per month.

## CHAPTER 2: IMPORTANT KEY ETSY STATS

- 34% run their creative businesses on Etsy as their sole source of income.
- **97%** of Etsy sellers run their businesses from home.
- **80%** of Etsy sellers identify as women.
- **1 in 4** Etsy sellers live in rural areas.
- The average age of Etsy sellers is **39.5 years**.
- **61%** of Etsy sellers sold for the first time on Etsy.
- **79%** of Etsy sellers consider their shop a business.

*[ My first try at Etsy was a complete failure. I ran my first shop and was only bringing in an average of just under $100 a month. Eventually, after about 4 months I decided to close it down. My goal back then was simply to make some extra money while doing something fun. I was bored with my full time job and wanted more. One important lesson I learned is that not every product or idea will sell. For example, if you create a product line targeting mosquito enthusiasts, don't expect huge returns. On the other hand, if your products cater to a broad audience like pet owners, you're likely onto something. It's much easier to market to a large, passionate group like pet lovers than to a niche with limited interest. ]*

- Gender (% identify as women): 82%
- Mean Age (years): 39.8
- Education (% college or more): 48%
- Median Household Income: $62,000
- Rural: 27%

*[ I'm a 50-year-old man with limited college education. I embarked on my Etsy journey in my early 40s when I launched my first shop. In 2018, I assisted my sister with optimizing and promoting her shop, and in 2019, I helped my best friend start his own shop. Neither my sister nor my friend*

*have extensive college backgrounds either yet both run hugely successful Etsy stores. ]*

- Etsy sellers spend 50% of their business time on making/designing and the rest on other administrative tasks.
- Sellers face major challenges in marketing their businesses (54%), as well as dealing with inconsistent sales (52%).
- 48% of Etsy sellers faced inflation and rising costs, with most seeing material and supply costs rise and nearly half seeing utility costs rise.

*[ I took a significant amount of time off to focus on my full-time job. After 1 year I decided to completely rebrand and relaunch my Etsy store. If you are in search of a new niche, here's a list of the most popular categories on the Etsy platform to help guide your choices ]*

## The top 10 most popular categories or niches on Etsy typically include:

1. **Jewelry:** Handmade and custom jewelry, including rings, necklaces, earrings, and bracelets.
2. **Clothing and Apparel:** Unique clothing items, such as custom t-shirts, dresses, and vintage apparel.
3. **Home Decor:** Items like wall art, pillows, candles, and personalized home accessories.
4. **Wedding Items:** Custom wedding invitations, favors, decorations, and bridal accessories.
5. **Craft Supplies and Tools:** Materials for crafting, including fabrics, beads, and DIY kits.
6. **Art and Collectibles:** Original paintings, prints, sculptures, and vintage collectibles.

7. **Personalized Gifts:** Customizable items like mugs, posters, and engraved keepsakes.
8. **Paper and Party Supplies:** Invitations, party decorations, planners, and stationery.
9. **Beauty and Personal Care:** Handmade soaps, skincare products, cosmetics, and bath accessories.
10. **Toys and Games:** Handmade or vintage toys, games, and educational kits for children.

Having a single theme or focusing on one category, such as jewelry or home decor, is important for an Etsy shop because it helps establish a clear brand identity and target a specific audience. When your shop has a cohesive theme, it becomes easier for potential buyers to understand what you offer and why they should choose your products. This focus also allows you to optimize your listings, keywords, and marketing strategies for a particular niche, improving your visibility in search results and attracting more relevant traffic. Additionally, a well-defined theme enhances customer trust and loyalty, as buyers are more likely to return to a shop that consistently offers products aligned with their interests and needs. By specializing in a single category, you can build a strong reputation, stand out in a crowded marketplace, and drive long-term success for your Etsy business.

*Action Step*: Decide on a theme for your shop, remove listings that don't fit and add new ones that do. Give your Etsy shop an identity and stick with it. You can always open another Etsy store later if you want to test out other themes.

*[ I reopened my Etsy shop with a fresh name, a new niche, and a strong determination to succeed. My revamped product line spanned several categories, including Home Decor, Wedding Items, and Art and Collectibles.*

*As you manage your Etsy shop, you'll find that many of your listings might overlap across different categories, as mine did. However, I recommend focusing your shop on a single theme or niche. A well-defined niche increases the likelihood that buyers will purchase multiple related items from you. Keep in mind, Etsy allows you to open multiple storefronts, so you can experiment with different niches or themes. At one point, I managed three separate shops, each catering to a different niche. ]*

# Chapter 3: The Etsy Brain - Decoding Etsy's Search Algorithm

Your entire approach to marketing your Etsy shop MUST be centered around understanding the Etsy's Search algorithm. Understanding the Etsy algorithm is crucial to succeeding in the Etsy marketplace because it directly impacts your shop's visibility and, ultimately, your sales. As you continuously monitor your Etsy stats you'll find that the majority of your shop's traffic will come from Etsy search (see Figure 3). Etsy's algorithm determines which products appear in search results, making it the gatekeeper between your shop and potential customers. If your listings aren't optimized to align with the algorithm's criteria—such as relevant keywords, listing quality, and customer engagement—they may get buried beneath thousands of competing products.

*Figure 3*

By mastering the algorithm, you can strategically position your products where they are most likely to be seen by interested buyers. This involves using the right keywords, creating high-quality listings, and maintaining positive customer interactions. But sometimes even that isn't enough. I'll explain in later chapters. When you understand how the algorithm works, you can make data-driven decisions to improve your shop's performance, ensuring that your products rank higher in search results. In a competitive marketplace like Etsy, this knowledge gives you a significant advantage, helping you attract more traffic, convert visitors into customers, and grow your business.

Etsy's algorithm can be understood through Etsy Search, which uses a combination of factors to determine product ranking in search results. Here are some of the key factors that can hugely impact the Etsy algorithm:

1. **Relevance:** The algorithm considers how well the product title, tags, and descriptions match the buyer's search terms. Keywords play a critical role here.
2. **Listing Quality Score:** This score is influenced by how often peo-

# CHAPTER 3: THE ETSY BRAIN - DECODING ETSY'S SEARCH ALGORITHM

ple click on your listings and make purchases. Higher engagement leads to better ranking.

3. **Customer and Market Experience Score:** Shops with positive reviews, a history of good customer service, and completed shop policies tend to rank higher.
4. **Recency of Listings:** New or recently updated listings may receive a temporary boost in search results, giving them a chance to gain traction.
5. **Shipping Price:** Offering free or competitive shipping can improve your ranking since Etsy prioritizes listings with attractive shipping terms.
6. **Conversion Rate:** Listings that convert well (i.e., turn views into sales) are more likely to be ranked higher.
7. **Listing Age:** Older listings may be deprioritized if they haven't generated interest over time, unless they're regularly updated or selling well.
8. **Etsy Ads:** Paying for Etsy Ads can boost your visibility in search results, although organic factors also play a significant role.

Etsy's algorithm is always evolving, adjusting to buyer behavior and marketplace trends, so it's crucial to keep optimizing your shop to maintain a strong product ranking. In the upcoming chapters, we'll explore these factors in detail. You'll find simple, actionable steps to fully optimize your shop before I reveal the main ingredient for The Etsy Seller's Secret Weapon.

# Chapter 4: Relevance

**Relevance** is one of the most critical factors that the Etsy algorithm considers when determining how your listings are ranked in search results. The concept of relevance revolves around how closely your listings match what potential buyers are searching for. In a marketplace as vast as Etsy, ensuring that your products are relevant to shoppers' search queries is essential for visibility, traffic, and ultimately, sales.

The Etsy algorithm aims to deliver the most appropriate results to buyers, so it places a heavy emphasis on relevance when ranking listings. Relevance is determined by how well your listing's titles, tags, categories, and attributes align with the search terms used by potential buyers. The more closely your listing matches a search query, the higher it is likely to appear in search results.

**Example: Keeping a Personalized Tumbler Listing Relevant**

While having a title like "Personalized Tumbler" is relevant, it may not be enough to ensure your listing stands out. To enhance visibility and attract more traffic, you should expand your title and add more popular keywords using insights from the Etsy Search tool. As discussed in Chapter 2, exploring alternative keyword phrases can significantly increase your listing's exposure.

CHAPTER 4: RELEVANCE

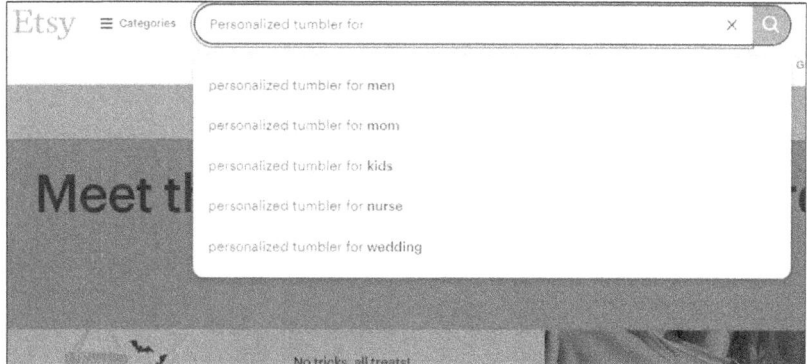

*Figure 4*

Expand your keywords with Etsy's Search bar (Figure 4). Start by typing "personalized tumbler for" into the Etsy Search bar without pressing Enter. Etsy will suggest popular search terms such as "personalized tumbler for mom," "personalized tumbler for dad," or "personalized tumbler for nurse." These suggestions indicate popular search queries and should be incorporated into your title and tags to capture a wider audience.

But don't stop there! Think about various occasions, holidays, or specific events that could be relevant. For example, "personalized tumbler for birthday gift" or "custom tumbler for Halloween" could attract buyers looking for gifts or seasonal items. By considering different buyer perspectives and adding these keywords to your title, you open up more opportunities for your product to be discovered.

It's crucial to include a range of popular, relevant key phrases in your title and tags, even if it makes the title seem a bit crowded. The goal is to ensure that the Etsy algorithm has ample opportunity to show your listing to potential buyers who might be searching for related products. Remember, the more specific and varied your keywords, the better your chances of capturing interest and driving traffic to your shop.

Etsy allows you to use up to 140 characters for your listing titles. This gives you ample space to include relevant keywords that can help your products be discovered in search results. So, use up all that space to fill up your title with popular keywords.

*[ Over time, I uncovered more and more key phrases that helped increase traffic to my listings by 10 times or more. I incorporated phrases like 'anniversary gifts for him,' 'wedding gifts for bride,' and 'personalized dad gifts.' I also experimented with more unconventional keywords such as '20th birthday gift for him' and 'boyfriend gift.' By adding various combinations of these key phrases into my titles and tags, I was able to significantly boost visibility and attract more potential buyers. ]*

Keywords in your listing title must also match the listing tags in your Etsy shop because this alignment maximizes your listing's relevance and visibility in search results. When the same keywords are used in both the title and tags, it reinforces to the Etsy algorithm that your listing is highly relevant to those search terms. This can improve your ranking, making it more likely that potential buyers will find your product when they search for those specific terms. Additionally, matching keywords help ensure that your listing appears in a wider range of related searches, increasing the chances of attracting the right audience. Etsy's algorithm may use any variation of your title and tags to show your listing to potential buyers.

**Action Step**: Give your listing a facelift. Add a new title and fill it up with popular and relevant keywords."

***Action Step***: Add all keywords used in the last action step and include them into your tags. Example tags you can add: "personalized tumbler", "best friend gift", "birthday gift", "boyfriend gift", "christmas gift", "tumbler for nurse", etc.

# Chapter 5: Quality and Customer & Market Experience Score

The **Quality Score** is vital in the Etsy algorithm because it reflects how well your listings perform in terms of customer engagement and satisfaction. This score is influenced by factors like click-through rates, conversion rates, and the overall buyer experience, including reviews and customer service. A high-quality score signals to Etsy that your listings are attractive, relevant, and trusted by buyers, which can lead to better visibility and higher placement in search results. Maintaining a strong quality score is essential for driving traffic, increasing sales, and sustaining long-term success on the platform. All the other factors in the Etsy algorithm impacts the quality score. So, this is just a reminder to take each part of the algorithm seriously.

## CHAPTER 5: QUALITY AND CUSTOMER & MARKET EXPERIENCE SCORE

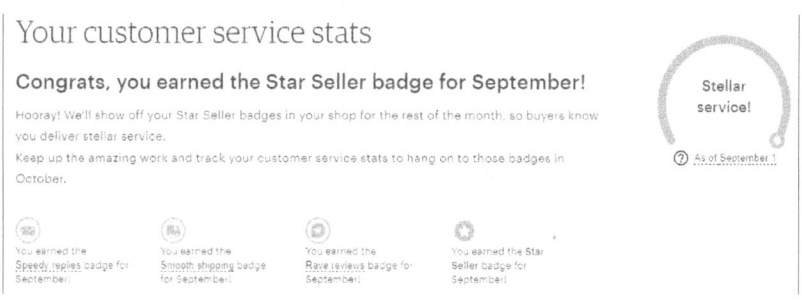

*Figure 5*

**Customer and Market Experience Score** is critical in the Etsy algorithm as it reflects the overall satisfaction and trustworthiness of your shop (Figure 5). This score is determined by factors like customer reviews, response times, completed shop policies, and adherence to Etsy's standards. A high score indicates that you provide excellent customer service, reliable shipping, and quality products, which boosts your shop's credibility. Etsy rewards shops with strong Customer and Market Experience Scores by giving them higher visibility in search results, leading to more traffic, better rankings, and increased sales.

Here are some helpful tips: always respond to customer messages within 24 hours, especially the initial inquiry, as failing to do so can negatively affect your shop's score. If a customer leaves a negative review, reach out right away to resolve the issue. Most buyers will revise or remove their review when they see you are attentive and willing to help. If a 3-star review or lower remains unchanged, you can leave a polite response explaining the situation and encouraging future customers to reach out with any issues. Also, be sure to ship orders within the time frame you've promised. If you specify a 3-day turnaround, stick to it. If that time frame becomes too difficult, be upfront and adjust it to something more manageable.

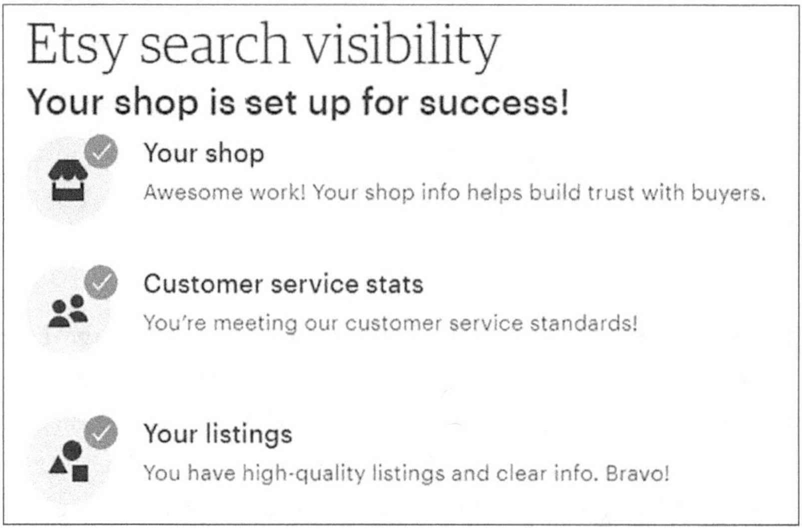

## Etsy search visibility
### Your shop is set up for success!

 **Your shop**
Awesome work! Your shop info helps build trust with buyers.

 **Customer service stats**
You're meeting our customer service standards!

 **Your listings**
You have high-quality listings and clear info. Bravo!

*Figure 6*

[ *I make it a priority to respond to all customer messages right away. To ensure they get a timely reply, I even set up Etsy's auto-reply feature. Failing to respond within 24 hours can quickly hurt your shop's rating. In my experience, it takes effort to receive less than a 5-star review, so there's no excuse. Keeping a 5-star rating is simple as long as you deliver on your promises and provide high-quality products (Figure 6).* ]

CHAPTER 5: QUALITY AND CUSTOMER & MARKET EXPERIENCE SCORE

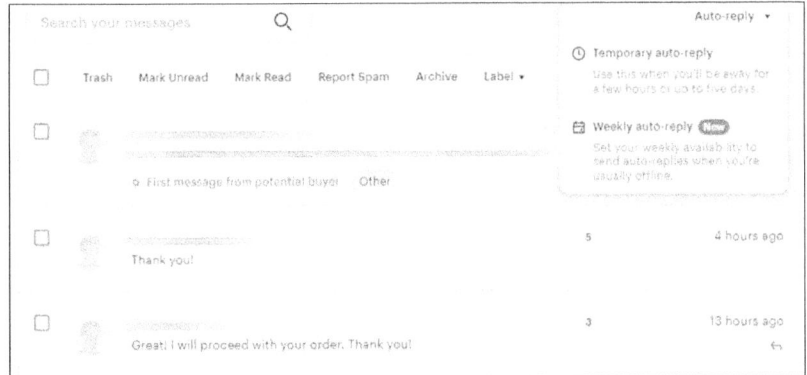

*Figure 7*

***Action Step***: Enable the Etsy Auto-reply feature so that all incoming messages are responded to instantly (Figure 7).

# Chapter 6: Recency of Listings and Listing Age

The recency of a listing is important in the Etsy algorithm because it helps fresh listings gain initial visibility and traction. When a product is newly listed or recently updated, Etsy gives it a temporary boost in search results, allowing it to be seen by more potential buyers. This initial exposure is crucial for gathering clicks and sales, which can improve the listing's long-term ranking. Regularly updating or renewing listings can keep them relevant and maintain their visibility, helping to attract consistent traffic and sales in a competitive marketplace.

**The Challenge of Old Listings**

Older listings can pose a challenge for Etsy sellers. As your products age, they may become less visible to buyers, especially if they haven't been updated or sold recently. This can lead to a situation where your shop's inventory is not performing as well as it could, simply because the listings are no longer receiving the attention they once did.

**How to Counter Old Listings**

Fortunately, there are several strategies you can use to counter the effects of aging listings and keep your shop fresh and competitive:

1. **Regularly Renew Listings:** Renewing a listing involves refreshing its recency by paying a small fee to have it relisted. This simple action can give your older products a new lease on life, restoring their visibility boost and helping them reappear higher in search results. Renewing listings regularly can be an effective way to maintain consistent traffic to your shop.
2. **Update Product Photos:** High-quality images are critical for attracting buyers. If your listing photos are outdated, consider updating them with fresh, professional images that reflect current trends and highlight your product's best features. New photos can breathe new life into an older listing, making it more appealing and increasing its chances of being featured in search results.
3. **Revise Titles and Descriptions:** Product titles and descriptions play a significant role in SEO and how Etsy's algorithm ranks your listings. If your older listings aren't performing well, try revising their titles and descriptions with updated keywords and more compelling copy. This not only helps improve your listing's relevance but also aligns it with current search trends, making it more likely to attract buyers.
4. **Create Seasonal or Trend-Based Updates:** Consider updating your listings to align with seasonal trends or holidays. For example, if you sell home decor, you could refresh your product descriptions and photos to feature seasonal colors or themes. This approach can make older listings feel new and relevant again, increasing their chances of being discovered by buyers.

By managing the age of your listings effectively—through updates, relisting, or periodic renewals—you can keep your products visible, drive consistent traffic, and increase your chances of making sales, which ultimately supports the long-term success of your Etsy shop.

*[ Before I learned the secrets to effectively promoting my listings, many of them sat with little to no traffic. They weren't optimized, and over time, they simply grew stale. But once I understood the importance of having a fresh and active listing, I duplicated my old listings, refreshed them with new titles and tags. That was my way of countering aged listings. ]*

## The Cost of Listing

Etsy charges a listing fee of $0.20 for each new listing. This fee is charged when you first publish the listing, and it covers a four-month period or until the item sells, or if you manually renew the listing, whichever comes first. If the item sells before the four months are up, the listing automatically renews, and another $0.20 fee is charged. These fees are consistent regardless of the item's price, so they are a predictable cost of doing business on Etsy.

*[ I've noticed that Etsy loves an active shop. I first opened my shop with 10 listings. I continued to add a few new listings per week until I reached nearly 200. To keep my shop active, I would renew some of the listings almost daily. In my mind I thought I was tricking the Etsy algorithm from thinking it's a new item or that the item just sold. I had a strong conviction to try anything to see if my shop would get any traction. I considered the listing fee as part of my marketing spend. I don't necessarily recommend doing this all the time because the costs add up and it's clearly not as strong as getting a sale. Once I started getting sales on my renewed listing, I stopped the manual renewing, because The Etsy algorithm would eventually rank that listing much higher. In any case, doing this set the tone for what I discovered later, as you'll find in Chapter 9: The Secret Weapon. ]*

***Action Step*:** When you publish a new listing, renew a listing or duplicate a listing try to do it during high traffic hours. The initial boost could get your listing seen by more potential buyers increasing your chance of getting a quick sale.

# Chapter 7: Shipping Price

Shipping policies and price play a crucial role in the success of your Etsy shop. They not only impact the customer experience but also significantly influence how the Etsy algorithm ranks your listings in search results. In today's competitive online marketplace, getting your shipping policies right—especially offering free shipping—can make a considerable difference in your shop's visibility and sales performance.

**The Importance of Offering Free Shipping**

One of the most effective ways to boost your visibility on Etsy is by offering free shipping, and of course, prompt shipping times. Etsy has made it clear that listings with free shipping are prioritized in search results, especially for buyers in the U.S. The reasoning behind this is simple: free shipping is a major factor in a customer's decision to purchase. It removes a common barrier to buying and can significantly increase your conversion rates. Don't underestimate the importance of shipping cost and delivery times. Etsy favors a shop that takes shipping and shipping costs seriously.

## CHAPTER 7: SHIPPING PRICE

*Figure 8*

*[ As soon as Etsy announced they were prioritizing listings with free shipping, I adjusted my listing price in order to offer free shipping shop wide. I wanted to make sure that I wasn't giving Etsy any reason to lower my shop's ranking. ]*

**<u>Action Step</u>**: Adjust the price of all your listings to include the shipping cost. Offer free shipping across all listings in your shop.

# Chapter 8: Conversion Rate

Conversion rates are a critical metric for any online business, and Etsy is no exception. In the simplest terms, your conversion rate on Etsy is the percentage of visitors who take the desired action, typically making a purchase, after viewing your listing. It's a direct indicator of how well your products resonate with potential buyers and how effectively your shop turns traffic into sales. Understanding and optimizing your conversion rates is not only essential for generating revenue but also plays a pivotal role in how the Etsy algorithm ranks your listings.

**Calculating the Conversion Rate**

On Etsy, your conversion rate is calculated by dividing the number of sales by the number of visits your shop or listing receives, then multiplying by 100 to get a percentage. For example, if 100 people visit your listing and 5 make a purchase, your conversion rate would be 5%. This number provides a clear picture of your shop's performance—specifically how well your product pages convince shoppers to buy.

**Why Conversion Rates Matter**

Conversion rates are a key factor that the Etsy algorithm considers when determining the ranking of your listings in search results. High conversion rates signal to Etsy that your listings are attractive and relevant to buyers. When your products consistently convert well, the algorithm interprets this as a sign of quality and demand, leading to higher placement in search results.

Conversely, low conversion rates can harm your shop's visibility. If your listings receive plenty of views but few sales, the algorithm might perceive them as less appealing or relevant to buyers. Over time, this can result in your listings being pushed down in search results, reducing their exposure to potential customers and making it even harder to generate sales.

**The Impact of Conversion Rates on Business Growth**

Conversion rates directly affect your revenue and growth potential on Etsy. A slight increase in your conversion rate can lead to a significant boost in sales. For example, increasing your conversion rate from 2% to 3% may not seem like a big jump, but it can result in a 50% increase in sales, assuming your traffic remains constant (Figure 9 - 10).

# THE ETSY SELLER'S SECRET WEAPON

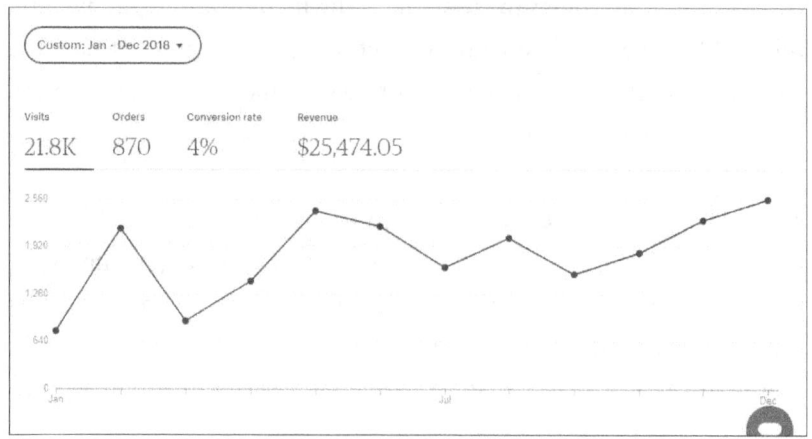

*Figure 9*

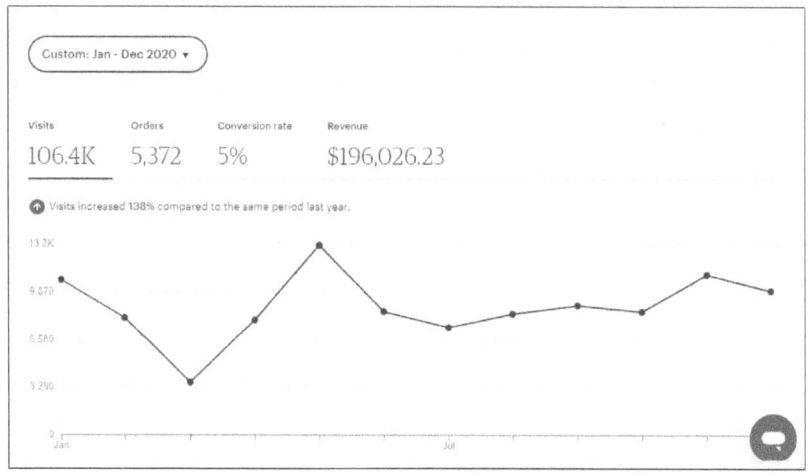

*Figure 10*

## CHAPTER 8: CONVERSION RATE

*[ My shop maintained an average conversion rate of 5%, peaking at 6.2% in a single month. But as I've mentioned before, a high conversion rate doesn't mean much if you're not driving enough traffic to your listings. Another important stat to track is the number of favorites your items receive. How many favorites do you get within a 30-day period? Focus on this for your higher-traffic listings. You can find this data on your dashboard's listings page (Figure 11). If a product is getting good traffic and plenty of favorites but no sales, it tells you two things: 1. People like the product, but 2. They think it's overpriced. ]*

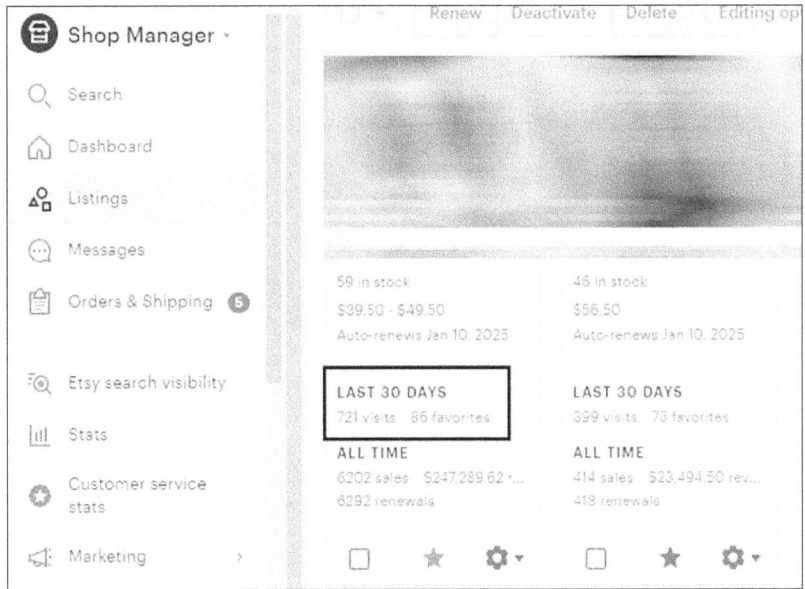

*Figure 11*

***Action Step:*** For listings that get a lot of favorites but few or no sales, try lowering the price gradually until you find that sweet spot where sales start coming in. For listings with low traffic and few favorites, you can either refresh them or leave them as they are. Every shop has a few listings that don't perform well, and that's okay—they won't negatively impact your shop's overall performance or rating.

# Chapter 9: The Secret Weapon

*Action Step*: Complete all previous action steps.

We've reached the final and most impactful step in The Etsy Seller's Secret Weapon. Now, this step does come with a cost—but not nearly as much as you might think. In fact, whatever number you have in mind, it's probably lower–much, much lower. Marketing is essential for running any successful business, and it usually requires a significant budget. The cost of marketing an Etsy shop, online store, or any eCommerce business varies based on your approach, the size of your shop, and your goals. In this chapter, I'll break down the typical marketing expenses you can expect, while showing you how to execute an even more effective strategy on a shoestring budget:

**Social Media Advertising Platforms** like Facebook, Instagram, Pinterest, TikTok can Cost: $5 - $50 per day.

**Search Engine Advertising (PPC) Platforms** like Google Ads or Bing Ads can Cost: $0.50 - $3 per click (on average).

**Etsy Promoted Listings** can cost: $1 - $3 per click (depending on competition).

**Influencer Marketing** can cost: $50 - $1,000+ per post or collaboration (depending on the influencer's reach).

**Content Marketing** (Blogs, Videos, etc.) can Cost: $100 - $1,000 per piece of content (written blogs, videos, graphics).

**SEO Services** can cost: $500 - $5,000 per month.

- **Considerations:** SEO is a long-term investment. Costs depend on the complexity of the website and the competitiveness of the industry.

**Software & Tools** can cost: $20 - $200 per month (for tools like analytics, keyword research, etc.).

**Total Monthly Budget Expectation**

- **Small Business/Etsy Shop:** $100 - $500.
- **Medium Business:** $500 - $2,000.
- **Large Business:** $2,000+.

You could easily pour hundreds of dollars a month into testing your shop's marketing efforts and still end up with no results. I strongly suggest you only use these strategies after your shop has a consistent stream of sales. On the other hand, the strategy outlined in this book allows you to test any listing on a tight budget, and you'll quickly discover if it's a hit or a miss. If it's a miss, don't sweat it—just move on and test the next listing. If it's a hit, you'll know much faster than with traditional marketing tactics. But remember, the action steps in this book are designed to build upon one another in order for the Secret Weapon to be complete and effective. Skipping any or all of the previous

## CHAPTER 9: THE SECRET WEAPON

action steps could leave you short of your goals. So, let's dive into the final *Action Step* of The Etsy Seller's Secret Weapon and bring it all together for success:

1. **Select Your Best Listing**: Start by choosing one of your most optimized listings, ideally one you believe has the highest potential to generate sales.
2. **Identify a Target Keyword Phrase**: Review the listing title and decide on a keyword phrase that you want to rank for on Etsy's first page. Choose a keyword that has the potential to attract significant traffic. For example, if your title is "Personalized Tumbler for Bridesmaids, Gift for Her, Birthday Gift for Friend," you might target a phrase like "Birthday Gift For Friend" or "Gift For Her." For this exercise, we'll focus on "Personalized Tumbler for Bridesmaids."
3. **Create a Promo Code**: Log into your Etsy seller dashboard, go to the Marketing tab, and select "Sales and Discounts." Create a promo code for 80% off or whatever maximum discount Etsy allows.
4. **Involve Your Network**: Contact a few close friends or family members who are willing to make a purchase from your shop using the promo code. You'll only need 2-3 people for this step. For steps 5-8, make sure to do these actions during Etsy's peak traffic hours (avoid late nights or early mornings).
5. **Renew the Listing**: Renew the chosen listing to give it a boost in Etsy's search results. This will cost you $0.20 but can improve visibility.
6. **Have One Person Search for Your Listing**: Ask one of your contacts to search for the target keyword phrase (e.g., "Personalized Tumbler for Bridesmaids") on Etsy. They may need to scroll through several pages of search results to find your listing. This

step is critical, so make sure they follow through as instructed.

7. **Click and Purchase**: Once they find your listing in the search results, have them click on it and complete the purchase using the promo code you provided. They can check out as a guest, but I recommend they create an Etsy account to leave a review later (see Step 11).
8. **Monitor for Organic Sales**: After the first purchase, wait a few hours to a day to see if the listing attracts an organic sale. If an organic sale occurs, proceed to Step 10. If no additional sales come in, go to Step 9.
9. **Second Purchase (If Necessary)**: If no sales occur after the first one, ask your second contact to repeat Steps 6-8.
10. **Request a Review**: After the sale is completed, remind your buyers to leave a positive review when Etsy allows it. They will need an Etsy account to leave a review. While guest checkout buyers can still leave a review, they'll need to create an account through a link sent by Etsy to complete this process.

Why does this strategy work? Etsy prioritizes and boosts listings that demonstrate strong sales performance, recognizing them as popular and desirable to buyers. When a listing consistently generates sales, under a specific keyword phrase, it signals to the Etsy algorithm that the product is in demand and well-received by customers, especially when a good review follows the purchase. As a result, the Etsy algorithm rewards these listings giving them more visibility in search results, making them more likely to appear on the first page. This increased exposure can create a positive feedback loop: the more a listing sells, the higher it ranks for certain keyword phrases, leading to even more sales. Some of these high-performing listings can maintain their position on the first page for extended periods, continuously attracting new buyers and driving significant traffic to the shop. This dynamic is why optimizing

CHAPTER 9: THE SECRET WEAPON

your listings for conversion and maintaining a strong sales record is essential for achieving and sustaining success on Etsy. Etsy will reward your shop's consistency with a "Star Seller!" badge (Figure 12).

*Figure 12*

*[ Before I discovered this game-changing strategy, I kept asking myself why certain listings always dominated the first page of Etsy search results. How could a new listing break through the clutter when the top spots were already filled? Then I realized—the listings at the top weren't just lucky; they were the most relevant and consistently sold, under popular phrases that Etsy's algorithm favored. Etsy's main goal is to generate sales, so naturally, they prioritize listings that are proven to sell. To get my own listings to climb the ranks, I had to align with Etsy's goals. I had to give the Etsy algorithm what it wanted. I enlisted the help of family and friends, because in Etsy's eyes, a sale is a sale, whether it comes from someone you know or a complete stranger.*

*At first, I experimented by buying my own listings and checking out as a guest, but I soon suspected that Etsy could track my activity through my IP address or device. That's when I focused on having others do a search and make purchases, which gave my listings an immediate boost. I discovered that Etsy rewards your entire shop when just a few of your products sell consistently. It was also a quick way to test new listings—if they didn't take off, I'd move on to the next. If they did, all it took was one purchase to trigger a chain reaction of sales through organic searches. This strategy gave my listings the traction they needed to stay relevant and visible. ]*

Now, you might be wondering, "How much is this strategy actually going to cost me?" Let's break it down step by step so you have a clear idea.

1. **Renewal Fees**: Every time you renew a listing (whether manually or automatically), Etsy charges you a $0.20 fee.
2. **Commission Fees**: Etsy also takes a 6.5% commission on the total sale price of every transaction. In this case, the commission is based on the discounted price after you apply your 80% promo code.

So, let's look at an example. If your listing price is $20 and you apply an 80% discount, here's the cost breakdown:

- **Listing Price After Discount**: $20 x 80% discount = **$4.00**
- **Etsy Commission**: 6.5% x $4 = **$0.26**
- **Renewal Fees**: $0.20 per renewal. Assuming you renew the listing twice (once before the purchase and once after), that's $0.20 x 2 = **$0.40**

**Total Cost**:

- Etsy Commission = **$0.26**
- Renewal Fees = **$0.40**

So, the total cost to run this strategy for one listing will approximately be **$0.66**. Now, if you apply this strategy to 4 other listings that also sell for $20 each, the total cost would be **$0.66 x 4 = $2.64—less than a**

## CHAPTER 9: THE SECRET WEAPON

**cup of coffee** to test multiple listings!

Everyone in your network that helped can be reimbursed, so the bottom line– this is simply a small investment in helping your listings rank higher and gain organic sales.

# Conclusion: The Journey Continues

Throughout this book, we've explored the key strategies and insider tactics that can transform your Etsy shop into a thriving business. We've covered everything from optimizing your listings and understanding Etsy's algorithm to discovering the true power of **The Etsy Seller's Secret Weapon**. Each step was designed to arm you with the tools you need to stand out in a crowded marketplace and drive real, sustainable results.

But knowing these strategies is just the beginning. The most important part is what you do next. It's one thing to read about how to optimize your shop or improve your conversion rates, but it's a completely different game when you put those strategies into action. Take the action steps you've learned, test them, and make them your own. Consistent effort is the fuel that will drive your success. Don't let this knowledge gather dust—use it, refine it, and watch your shop evolve.

Remember, every successful Etsy seller started exactly where you are now: with a dream and a willingness to learn. I've shared my journey with you to show that success doesn't come overnight, but it **does** come to those who stay committed. When I reopened my Etsy shop after a long hiatus, I wasn't sure how it would go, but by applying the strategies in this book, I turned my failure into success. You can do the same.

# CONCLUSION: THE JOURNEY CONTINUES

As you continue your Etsy journey, know that it's not a one-time effort but a continuous process of learning, optimizing, and evolving. The algorithm will change, trends will shift, and new challenges will arise. But the principles you've learned here will always hold true—stay relevant, focus on your customers, and keep optimizing.

**Take Action Now**

Your next step is clear: go back to your shop, pick one listing to start with, and apply everything you've learned. Choose your keyword phrase, renew that listing, and get ready to execute the final steps of **The Etsy Seller's Secret Weapon** strategy. By taking action today, you're already ahead of the game.

Success on Etsy isn't reserved for the few at the top. It's there for those who commit, adapt, and put in the work. You've already come this far—don't stop now. Every sale, every listing favorite, and every positive review brings you one step closer to building a shop that thrives.

**The Journey Continues**

This book marks the end of one chapter but the beginning of a much larger journey. You've learned the strategies to give your shop the boost it needs, and now it's up to you to apply them and keep pushing forward. Keep testing, keep optimizing, and most importantly, never stop learning. The success of your Etsy shop is within reach, and with **The Etsy Seller's Secret Weapon**, you have everything you need to take it to the next level.

Success doesn't come from luck—it comes from hard work and smart strategy. You've got both in your hands now, so go make it happen.

***Action Step:*** grab yourself a cup of coffee (Figure 13)!

*Figure 13*

# Resources

Mucenieks, A. (2024a, April 10). *What Is a Good Conversion Rate on Etsy?* Printify. Retrieved September 11, 2024, from https://printify.com/blog/what-is-a-good-conversion-rate-on-etsy/

Yaqub, M. (2024c, July 31). *Etsy Statistics: Sellers, Buyers, & More (Latest Data)*. Contimod. Retrieved September 11, 2024, from https://www.contimod.com/etsy-statistics/

Haleem, A. (2024b, February 22). *Etsy marks highest-ever annual revenue in 2023*. Digital Commerce 360. Retrieved September 11, 2024, from https://www.digitalcommerce360.com/2024/02/22/etsy-revenue-highest-ever-annual-q4-2023/

www.ingramcontent.com/pod-product-compliance
Lightning Source LLC
Chambersburg PA
CBHW051535240526
45471CB00020B/2939